Citizens of Hope

April,
2016

THE BASICS

Citizens of Hope:
Basics of Christian Identity

978-1-5018-1309-2 *Study Book*

978-1-5018-1310-8 *eBook*

978-1-5018-1311-5 *Leader Guide*

978-1-5018-1312-2 *Leader Guide eBook*

The Road to Amazing:
Basics of Christian Practice

978-1-5018-1313-9 *Study Book*

978-1-5018-1314-6 *eBook*

978-1-5018-1315-3 *Leader Guide*

978-1-5018-1316-0 *Leader Guide eBook*

Get in the Game:
Basics of Christian Service

978-1-5018-1317-7 *Study Book*

978-1-5018-1318-4 *eBook*

978-1-5018-1319-1 *Leader Guide*

978-1-5018-1320-7 *Leader Guide eBook*

For more information, visit www.AbingdonPress.com

The
BASICS

Citizens of
HOPE

basics of christian identity

Clayton Oliphint
and
Mary Brooke Casad

Abingdon Press
Nashville

Citizens of Hope
The Basics of Christian Identity

This book is printed on elemental chlorine-free paper.
ISBN 978-1-5018-1309-2

16 17 18 19 20 21 22 23 24 25—10 9 8 7 6 5 4 3 2 1
MANUFACTURED IN THE UNITED STATES OF AMERICA

To our family of origin—
our parents, Ben and Nancy Oliphint,
and our brothers, Stuart and Kelley Oliphint—
who lovingly shaped our identities
as citizens of hope.

CONTENTS

About the Authors

Clayton Oliphint and **Mary Brooke Casad** are siblings who share a passion for discipleship and helping others grow as followers of Jesus Christ. They grew up in four United Methodist congregations in Louisiana and Texas where their father, the late Ben Oliphint, was pastor. Following his election to the episcopacy in 1980, he served the Topeka and Houston areas. Both Clayton and Mary Brooke are married to fellow "preacher's kids" who share their rich heritage of faith and ministry.

Clayton is senior pastor of First United Methodist Church in Richardson, Texas, a church of six thousand members. He received his undergraduate degree from Austin College and a Master of Divinity and Doctor of Ministry from Perkins School of Theology. He and his wife, Lori, are the parents of three children. Beyond his church and local community involvement, he serves on the steering committee of the Office of Christian Unity and Interreligious Relationships of The United Methodist Church and as a director of the Texas Methodist Foundation Board.

Mary Brooke is former Executive Secretary of the Connectional Table of The United Methodist Church. She served as Director of Connectional Ministries in the Dallas area from 1997 to 2007. Currently, she is a trustee and past chair of the Foundation for Evangelism and a director of the Texas Methodist Foundation Board. She has a degree in journalism from Southern Methodist University and is the author of several *Bluebonnet the Armadillo* children's books, written to teach Texas children about their rich local heritage. She and her clergy husband, Vic, have two sons, a daughter-in-law, and three grandchildren. They live in Sulphur Springs, Texas.

Clayton and Mary Brooke are coauthors of The Basics series. Drawing on their rich faith heritage, they write with a warm storytelling approach that resonates and helps make practical connections between faith and action.

INTRODUCTION

We're all familiar with filling out forms—whether for school, work, travel, or recreation; no doubt you've completed countless forms over the course of your life. Standard forms ask for information such as your name, address, city, state, zip code, phone number, e-mail address, Social Security number, race, and nationality—all for the purpose of identifying who you are.

Recently I **(Clayton)** was filling out a form for a new passport. As I came to the line marked "Race" and searched for the appropriate category, I remembered the Scripture I had preached the previous Sunday:

> *But you are a chosen race, a royal priesthood, a holy nation, God's own people, in order that you may proclaim the mighty acts of him who called you out of darkness into his marvelous light.*
> *(1 Peter 2:9)*

My mind began to wander, and I found myself daydreaming about who we are as followers of Christ. What is our true identity? This is the question Mary Brooke and I will be exploring with you in this study.

Imagine if we filled out forms in a way that indicated our identity in Christ.

What is our race? According to 1 Peter 2:9, we are a "chosen race...God's own people." So what if beside the word *Race* we wrote simply "child of God"? If asked to explain which God, we might elaborate and say, "The God who raised his Son, Jesus Christ." Each of us is a child of this God, who has been revealed in the life, death, and resurrection of Jesus Christ. What a heritage!

What is our state? Because of what God has done, we are living in a state of grace. Mary Brooke and I are proud of the state of our birth, Louisiana, and Texas, the state where we have both resided for more than four decades. You have your own roots and ties to one or more states. But on a spiritual level, we all are living in a state of grace. As 1 Peter 2:10 reminds us: "Once you had not received mercy, but now you have received mercy." Yes, God has been gracious and merciful, and we are so thankful to live in grace.

What is our nationality? We are proud to be American citizens and to enjoy the freedoms for which many have given so much—even their lives—to protect. Perhaps you share this citizenship or call another beloved country your home. But on a spiritual level, our citizenship is broader than our country of birth or chosen nationality. Because of God's gift of resurrection, we are citizens of hope. We are resurrection people, those who are well-acquainted with suffering and death, but who know that God is never finished with us. When we go through various trials and tribulations, we face those times with hope. This hope is not our own wishful optimism—it is deeply grounded in the life, death, and resurrection of Jesus Christ. As his followers, Jesus' story becomes our story.

In *Citizens of Hope*, one of three studies in The Basics series, our purpose is to remind us of our true identity as people of hope. Throughout the centuries Christians have been citizens of hope, standing in the dark places of life and proclaiming that God is still alive and working in the world. We, too, are called to be citizens of hope in our world today. There are those predicting the end of the church and those predicting the end of the world, but as citizens of hope, we know the story is not over. God is a God of resurrection, and God is about the work of bringing new life to the church and the world. Our role is to point to the God of resurrection, to "proclaim the mighty acts of him who called [us] out of darkness into his marvelous light."

We pray that as you read these chapters, the reality of your true identity will become apparent to you and to those around you. You are a child of God, living in a state of grace—a full-fledged citizen of hope!

—**Clayton Oliphint** and **Mary Brooke Casad**

HOW TO USE THIS BOOK

Citizens of Hope is one of three small-group studies in The Basics, a discipleship series that explores the basics of living as a follower of Jesus. Each study may be done separately or as part of a twelve-week course. Some congregations may choose to use one or all three studies as a churchwide study series.

This book is designed for you, the group member. Each week you will read one chapter and then gather with your group for discussion. (A leader guide with session outlines and other helps is available separately.) If desired, you also may use this book as a personal devotion guide. Before reading each chapter, offer a prayer and invite God's presence and wisdom as you seek to claim your identity as a citizen of hope.

Our approach throughout is to write on a very personal and practical level, speaking with a unified voice, except when sharing our individual stories (these are identified by our names, which appear in bold within parentheses). Our hope is that as you read you will feel you are traveling with friends, fellow citizens of hope who are making the journey along with you.

Each chapter begins with a passage of Scripture, followed by several short thematic readings. At the end of the chapter, you will find a Reflect section where you can record your thoughts in response to specific questions. Drawing on the imagery of a citizen of hope who is making a journey, in this reflection time you will be guided by the following:

⚓ Port of Entry

A port of entry is defined as a place where persons or goods enter a country. As Christians, our "port of entry" is Holy Scripture. This is the place from which our study and inquiry begin. Each chapter is based on a passage of Scripture, which is printed at the beginning of the chapter. The Port of Entry section invites you to reflect further on the Scripture passage.

✍ Customs Declaration Form

A customs declaration form is a statement showing goods that are being imported. Citizens must declare the goods they are bringing with them into a country, primarily because such goods may require a duty payment. This section invites you to reflect on the insights you gained from each section of the chapter and "declare" the learnings that are significant for you. (Don't worry; your declarations are "duty free"!)

✦ Passport Stamp

Upon entering or exiting a country, one's passport is stamped, serving as a record of the passport holder's visit. Passport stamps invoke memories of special trips. This section invites you to share what is "stamped" on your heart from the chapter. What was most memorable? Was it a passage of Scripture, a story, or a statement? This is an opportunity to write down your main "takeaway" from the chapter.

Your responses to these prompts will help you make personal application and will prepare you for sharing with your small group.

As you make your way through this book—whether you are reading it as part of a small-group study or as a personal devotion guide—we hope you will find encouragement and inspiration for your discipleship journey.

CHAPTER 1

IDENTITY CRISIS

Hope in Tough Times

But now thus says the LORD,
he who created you, O Jacob,
he who formed you, O Israel:
Do not fear, for I have redeemed you;
I have called you by name, you are mine.
When you pass through the waters, I will be with you;
and through the rivers, they shall not overwhelm you;
when you walk through fire you shall not be burned,
and the flame shall not consume you.
For I am the LORD your God,
the Holy One of Israel, your Savior.
I give Egypt as your ransom,
Ethiopia and Seba in exchange for you.
Because you are precious in my sight,
and honored, and I love you,
I give people in return for you,
nations in exchange for your life.
Do not fear, for I am with you;
I will bring your offspring from the east,
and from the west I will gather you;
I will say to the north, "Give them up,"
and to the south, "Do not withhold;
bring my sons from far away
and my daughters from the end of the earth—
everyone who is called by my name,
whom I created for my glory,
whom I formed and made...."
I am about to do a new thing;
now it springs forth, do you not perceive it?
I will make a way in the wilderness
and rivers in the desert.

(Isaiah 43:1-7, 19)

20

IDENTITY CRISIS

Hope in Tough Times

Identity theft is a big issue in our modern world. Countless people have been robbed of their identities through credit card fraud, and almost every day there is a news story about some company or organization whose information has been hacked by online predators. Personal identities are stolen and private information is exposed, and this sometimes results in a financial or personal price tag that can be costly.

(Clayton) I know what it is like to have my identity stolen. It happened several years ago when my credit card information was stolen. Fortunately, my credit card company was suspicious of the large purchases being made in another state and took a closer look. They recognized that my identity—or, in their view, my spending habits—did not match the transactions they were seeing.

Losing your identity—or having your identity stolen—is a traumatic experience. I have a friend who was the team leader on a mission trip outside the United States and lost his passport while abroad. Officials at the American embassy had to make calls back to the United States to verify his physical description before he could obtain papers that allowed him to return home. He told me about the experience, "Do you know how hard it is to establish your identity when you have no credentials and no way of proving who you are? Do you know how hard it is to prove who you are when you have no proof of who you are?"

In life, sometimes it's as if we lose our citizenship papers and we are left without an identity. Unlike my friend, who knew who he was and had to convince the authorities of his identity, tough times can cause us to forget who and *Whose* we are. We forget that we are citizens of hope, and that the Bible has given us our papers, our identity.

In Isaiah 43:1-7, we see the prophet Isaiah telling his people that they had lost their identity—and that they had also forgotten something about God's identity. These people of one nation, now living in another nation, had lost the sense of who they were. Much of the Bible was written during this time known as the Exile, which actually refers to two different times of captivity in the history of Israel and Judea. Twice they were overcome by foreign empires who crushed them, knocked down their Temple, and took them away. And what did they forget when they were in a foreign land? They forgot who and Whose they were. The people were asking, "Where's God? Why did God allow this bad thing to happen to us? How did we end up here? How can we worship God in a strange land? We don't even know who we are anymore."

It was during that time of exile that people began to say, "We need to write these stories down for our children. We need to record these stories so that our children will not forget." Isaiah spoke to this situation as a prophet of God, reminding the people of their true identity as citizens of hope. In addition to remembering who they were, he also wanted them to remember who God was and that God was not finished with them yet.

(Mary Brooke) When we were growing up, our mother had a unique way of reminding us of our identity. My husband, Vic, experienced this on our very first date. As we left the house, my mother bid us goodbye and said, "Remember the Alamo!" Then, from another room in the house, my grandmother called, "Remember the Alamo!" Finally, my little brother Kelley ran to the door and called, "Remember the Alamo!"

When we got in the car, Vic said, "I don't understand what's going on. Didn't you grow up in Louisiana? What's with the Texas history?"

Knowing his history well, Vic remembered that, in 1836, Texas was fighting for its independence from Mexico when a famous battle occurred at the Alamo mission in San Antonio. History records that all 179 defenders of the Alamo perished in the battle against five thousand Mexican troops. The cry "Remember the Alamo!" became the cry of the Texans in subsequent battles, as they paid homage to the fallen heroes and encouraged one another on to victory.

My grandmother had grown up in Texas before she married and moved to Louisiana, and, for some reason, had adopted the phrase as a family mantra. When my mother was young, every time she left the house, my grandmother would remind her to "Remember the Alamo!" My mother continued the tradition with her children, as I did with mine.

Though it had not been expressed in words, somehow I intuitively knew that the phrase "Remember the Alamo!" was a code. So on that first date with my future husband, I explained that the code meant this: "Remember who you are. Remember that you are a part of this family, and you are loved. Remember that to be a part of the family means that you have been given a great gift of identity, and with it comes great expectations of how you honor and use that gift."

It is essential that we remember who and Whose we are.

It is essential that
we remember who
and Whose we are.

You Are a Child of God

At the beginning of chapter 43, Isaiah says: "Thus says the LORD, / he who created you, O Jacob, / he who formed you, O Israel: / Do not fear, for I have redeemed you; / I have called you by name, you are mine" (v. 1). You belong to God. That's who you are. You are a child of God.

Have you ever wondered who you are? Every major, significant change in our lives brings about an identity crisis. When we go through change, we ask the question, "Now that this is the situation in my life, who am I now?" And because change is constant, we are constantly being challenged with an identity crisis. We forget who we are. One of the reasons we worship together in a community of faith is to remind ourselves that we belong to God.

We have an identity that has been given to us. As Christians, we have claimed that identity. That identity was given to us at our baptism. In baptism, the water symbolizes an outward and visible sign of something that is true on the inside. Our true identity is that we are children of God.

Though this identity is affirmed at our baptism, it often escapes our focus in everyday living. Sometimes we feel that we do not measure up to others around us, and this comparison starts early in life for many of us. In school there are other children who seem to be smarter, richer, funnier, more popular, more athletic—and on and on it goes. This sense of not being enough—of being less than—leads us to feel insecure, and this insecurity drives us to try to be something that we are not in an effort to prove ourselves to others. It continues into our teen and adult years as we unfairly measure ourselves against others by the jobs we hold, the money we make, the clothes we wear, the places we live, the way we look, and so forth. Some of the worst decisions we make in life are driven by feelings of inadequacy and insecurity. This is why it is so important for parents and the faith community to help every child have a secure sense of identity as a child of God. It is equally important for us as adults to claim this gift of identity that God gives us. It is so easy to forget who we really are.

So when you go through tough times and forget who you are, remember that the Bible tells you who you are: a child of God. It tells you not only who you are but also Whose you are. You are a child of God. This is your true identity.

God didn't make a mistake when making you. You were made in God's image. You are beautiful in God's sight. Have you ever thought about that? Now, the world might tell you something about who you are and what you look like. But the Bible tells each one of us that God looks at us as a work of art. You are beautiful in God's sight just as you are. God loves you and has called you by name. This is God's word to you: "You are mine."

(Mary Brooke) When I was a very young child, my parents and I often visited Mrs. Howard and her son, Nolan, who were memebers of our church. Mrs. Howard was quite elderly and usually in bed, so we would bring groceries or home-cooked meals to her house. Though she was unable to be up and around very much, she was always glad to see us. Nolan was different from anyone I had ever met, and I remember being a bit frightened of him at first. Then a middle-aged man, he had been born with physical and mental challenges. He didn't speak or see well, and he walked with a cane. But he was gentle and friendly, and soon we developed a special friendship. I remember that he delighted in giving me a piece of candy or a penny. And I was delighted by his smile and his gifts.

Only a few years after our visits began, Mrs. Howard and Nolan both died—one shortly after the other. I remember the sorrow and loss I felt when my parents shared the sad news of their deaths. That was one of my earliest experiences of death.

Years later, when I was pregnant with my first child, I had a conversation with my mother about how pregnancy was bringing me new insights. I had a new appreciation for each person I saw because each person was "somebody's child." I had a new understanding of what it meant to carry a little being within you for nine months, to give birth to a baby whom you loved long before you could even look at or hold that child. Surely, I told her, this must be the way God looks at every human being who has ever been born.

My mother looked thoughtful for a moment and then said, "Do you remember Nolan?"

I nodded yes. We had not spoken of him in many years, but he was etched deeply within my memory.

"I remember having similar insights about Mrs. Howard and Nolan," she said. "Even though Nolan was a grown man, he was 'somebody's child.' He was Mrs. Howard's little boy. And she loved him deeply."

I have long remembered that conversation with my mother. No matter who we are, what we look like, what abilities or disabilities we have, or how old we are, we are all "somebody's child." And that somebody loves us forever. Understanding this about human parents helps us begin to grasp the love that our heavenly Parent has for us.

What if we all looked at each other as "somebody's child"? What if we all looked at each other as "God's child"?

God Is With Us

The second word Isaiah spoke to the people in exile is a word that God speaks to all of us when we feel disconnected from God: "I am with you." Not only had the people lost a sense of their own identity, they had failed to grasp some basic truths about God's identity. Central to God's identity is God's promise to be with God's people. Isaiah reminded the people: "When you pass through the waters, I will be with you; / and through the rivers, they shall not overwhelm you; / when you walk through the fire you shall not be burned, / ...For I am the LORD your God, / ...Do not fear, for I am with you" (Isaiah 43:2-3a, 5a).

Over and over again, this is the Bible's message, for much of the Bible speaks to this question: Why do bad things happen to good people? In other words, why do people find themselves in exile?

We can reason things out to a certain degree; there is cause and effect. If this happens, then this is going to happen. If I text while I'm driving, then there could be dire consequences. Not just for me, but for others. Cause and effect. But there are some things that happen in life that defy explanation. There are things that happen to us and to people we love, and we wonder, *Why in the world do these things happen to these good people?* It makes no sense. And perhaps the Bible never fully and satisfactorily answers that question.

Here is what the Bible does tell us: God is with us. God says, "I am with you." When you go through these things you don't understand, when you go through the tough times, when you go through the fiery trials or the raging waters, God says, "I am with you." God's answer to the question *Why?* is a relationship. We may not ever understand why bad things happen to good people. But this is our certainty and, therefore, our hope: *God is with us!*

(Clayton) When my daughter Katy was about five years old, she and I were running errands one day and driving around town. A favorite song of mine came on the classic rock radio station I was listening to. (As a parent, I feel it is my duty to teach my kids about the finer things in life!) So I told Katy, "This is one of Daddy's favorite songs." I turned up the radio and started blasting out that hit song from the Doobie Brothers, "Jesus Is Just Alright with Me." Who could forget those classic lyrics?

> *Jesus is just alright with me,*
> *Jesus is just alright, oh yeah.*[1]

Later that evening at home, I heard Katy in the other room singing that song at the top of her lungs, but somehow she had misunderstood the lyrics and was singing:

> *Jesus stays up all night with me,*
> *Jesus stays up all night, oh yeah.*

Well, she misunderstood the lyrics, but her theology was sound!

Jesus is with us, and he stays up all night with us on all those days that end in the question, *Why?* What percentage of the time is God with us? One hundred percent. In other words: all of the time. God's presence is God's answer, reminding us, "I am with you. You are not alone."

(Clayton) Several years ago I began to pay attention to the words of the prayers I was saying for people. I became aware that when I prayed for others, I often would use phrases such as, "God, please be with Jim today as he faces surgery," or, "God, please be with Cathy as she grieves the death of her father." Suddenly I was convicted by the realization that God was already there! God has promised to be with us in all circumstances and situations. This realization radically altered my prayer life.

Now, when praying for others, my prayers are more like this: "God, I know that you are with Jim as he faces surgery today. Please help him to recognize your presence with him to give him strength and assurance," or "God, thank you for being with Cathy as she grieves the loss of her father. Help her to feel and experience your presence and your comforting peace." What a difference it makes in our prayer lives when we claim that God is already with us!

One of the last things Jesus said to his disciples was, "Remember, I am with you always" (Matthew 28:20). He didn't say, "When it's convenient or when everything is going great in your life, then you will know that I'm there." He said, "I am with you always." That may be the most important word we can communicate as people of faith to this world. We need to proclaim this word to people who feel all alone, people who feel they have no citizenship, people who feel they have no sense of rootedness: God is with them. When we hear people say, "Where is God?" or "God was not with me that day," or "I feel distant from God," we can respond, "No, friend. God is with you always. That's the Bible's promise. God is with you always."

(Mary Brooke) I will never forget the day that our father had a heart attack shortly after his eighty-third birthday. My brothers and I rushed to the hospital as he underwent several medical procedures. Within a few days, he seemed to be on the road to recovery, so my brothers left to return to their homes, and I stayed to be with my mother. However, within a matter of hours, my father's condition changed. We were standing by his bedside when the monitors indicated his heart had stopped beating. Medical staff rushed into the room, and a nurse whisked my mother and me into a waiting room. In stunned silence, we hugged each other. I quickly called my brothers to let them know what was happening. As I spoke to Clayton, I asked, "Can you pray with us?" There was silence, and then he said in a choked voice, "I have no words." We hung up.

Five seconds later Clayton called me back.

"God is with us," he said. "God is with us."

When we have no words, God gives us the Word: *Emmanuel*, God with us.

God Makes a Way Out of No Way

There's one more thing Isaiah tells the people in exile about this God of hope: God will make a way out of no way. He says it so beautifully in Isaiah 43:19:

> *I am about to do a new thing;*
> *   now it springs forth, do you not perceive it?*
> *I will make a way in the wilderness*
> *   and rivers in the desert.*

God will make a way when it seems there is no way.

When we have no words,
God gives us the Word:
Emmanuel, God with us.

In Jim Collins's business bestseller *Good to Great*, there's a fascinating section about "The Stockdale Paradox." Admiral Jim Stockdale, the highest-ranking prisoner of war in the Vietnam War, spent eight years of his life in a prison known as the "Hanoi Hilton." Most of that time he was in solitary confinement.

Collins interviewed Admiral Stockdale, asking him about his experiences. Stockdale responded that, even though at the time he had no way to know how or when his imprisonment would end, he never lost faith in the end of the story. He never doubted that he would get out, that he would prevail, and that his horrible experience would be the defining event of his life. And then Collins asked him about the prisoners who didn't make it out. Stockdale said: "The optimists . . . they were the ones who said, 'we're going to be out by Christmas.' And Christmas would come, and Christmas would go. Then they'd say, 'We're going to be out by Easter.' And Easter would come, and Easter would go. And then Thanksgiving, and then it would be Christmas again. And they died of a broken heart."[2]

Stockdale continued, "This is a very important lesson. You must never confuse faith that you will prevail in the end—which you can never afford to lose—with the discipline to confront the most brutal facts of your current reality, whatever they might be."[3]

That is why each of us needs something deeper than optimism. When you are going through a tough time in life, you must face the brutal facts of your situation. But here is the paradox: you do so with an unwavering hope because you know the end of the story.

As Christians, we know where that hope comes from. That hope comes not from our wishful thinking or our optimism but from God's presence, reassuring us, "You are mine; I am with you; I will make a way out of no way." We have a God who is with us in the midst of every situation, giving us a solid foundation of hope for tough times.

The world needs to know that there is a God who can take the worst of situations and help us face those situations head on. This may be the reality of where we are today, but we don't have to stay there, because God is not planning for us to stay there. God is making a way for us when it seems there is no way to move forward. God is already at work in our lives preparing the way. The prophet Jeremiah said it this way: "For surely I know the plans I have for you, says the LORD, plans for your welfare and not for harm, to give you a future with hope" (Jeremiah 29:11).

(Clayton) I met Karen when she was a single mother. She'd been divorced for five years, at the lowest point of her life after losing a job and going through financial ruin. She was working hard in the midst of that situation to raise her son and do what she could do to pull out of the despair and hopelessness she often felt. One day her ten-year-old son accidentally threw a baseball through her window. She threw up her hands and said, "Just one more thing." She didn't have much money, but she called a repairman, Chris, who came to the house and replaced the window. Karen and Chris had a nice conversation, and sparks began to fly. Soon they began dating.

Eighteen months later, Chris and Karen stood before me at a church altar and got married. Karen proclaimed about how, in the midst of her exile, in the midst of her deepest, darkest times, God was already at work preparing a way for her, preparing her to experience hope beyond that despair. God was already at work doing that.

Never doubt that, on your worst days, God is already at work preparing you for something more. God works best when things are at their worst. That's what the Resurrection tells us. When this whole world looked as if it had lost its mind and crucified the Messiah, when the world was its darkest, guess what God was doing? God was already at work raising up his Son, preparing the world for hope.

Reclaim your citizenship today! You have your papers. The Bible tells you who you are. You are a child of God. No longer do you need to suffer with an identity crisis. What would it mean for you today to receive again that identity—child of God—as a gift from God? Every day the world is trying to tell you who you are, but you know better! You are a child of God. God is with you. You are not alone. What difference would it make in your life today and every day to claim this truth?

God is making a way out of no way—for every one of us. What would it mean for you to accept that truth? Whatever you are facing this day, face it head on. It is reality. But know this: God is not finished with you. You may be overwhelmed by the reality you are facing today. It may be causing you great despair. But God is already working in your life to write the next chapter.

Through Isaiah's words, God reminded the Hebrew people of their true identity as God's own beloved children. God also reminded them of who God is and what God is up to in the world. God's presence with them and promise to restore them made all the difference in helping them understand their identity. They may have been far from home, but they knew this truth: they were citizens of hope. And we are too!

Gracious and loving God, I give you thanks for this day of life. I am your child, and I am grateful for the many ways you have shown that truth to me. Forgive me when I forget my true identity as your child. I have far too often allowed the world to tell me who I am; and Lord, unfortunately, I have listened and believed that voice rather than your voice. Speak to my heart today. Remind me that I belong to you, that I matter to you. You are with me. No matter what obstacle I face today, help me to remember that you will be with me and already are at work preparing a way forward. Because of you and what you've done for me through Jesus Christ, I am a citizen of hope. In Jesus' name I pray. Amen.

REFLECT

⚓ Port of Entry

Reread Isaiah 43: 1-7, 19 (see page 20).

Isaiah was writing to people who had lost their identity and thus their hope. Their land had been overtaken and their kingdom crushed. People had been carried off into exile, and now they cried the tears of the hopeless: "How could we sing the Lord's song / in a foreign land?" (Psalm 137:4). Their religious identity was so closely tied to their land that this move away from their land had caused a real identity crisis. They had forgotten who they were and *Whose* they were.

Has there been a time when you forgot your true identity? How has God helped you understand your identity?

Reading this book, so far, is reminding me of "whose" I am.

✍ Customs Declaration Form

What insights did you gain from each section?

You Are a Child of God

*Yes, we forget from
Time to Time, but am now*

God Is With Us *reminded + aware*

God Makes a Way out of No Way *My Son.*

*God is making a
new way for Tim.*

⊛ Passport Stamps

What is "stamped" on your heart that you will remember most from this chapter?

I belong to God.

CHAPTER 2

A VISION OF HOPE

Therefore, since we have been declared righteous by faith,
we have peace with God through our Lord Jesus Christ,
through whom we have also obtained access by faith into
this grace in which we stand, and we rejoice in the hope of
God's glory. Not only this, but we also rejoice in sufferings,
knowing that suffering produces endurance, and
endurance, character, and character, hope. And hope does
not disappoint, because the love of God has been poured out
in our hearts through the Holy Spirit who was given to us.
(Romans 5:1-5 NET)

CHAPTER 2

A VISION OF HOPE

How do you see your life? Have you ever considered that we each have a unique perspective of our own life and the world in which we live? Have you ever noticed how quickly that perspective changes when we face obstacles or setbacks? This is one reason we need a framework that is constant, tried, and true—an unwavering viewpoint in the midst of an ever-changing and ever-challenging world.

(Clayton) For several years I have been struggling with my vision and what to do about it. Reading glasses were a bother because I had to perch them on my nose in order to read and then look over them to see people. This frustrated me, so I decided to try contact lenses. I went through several evolutions of different lenses. With the first lenses, sometimes I could see clearly when I was reading the Bible, but people seated in the back of the church looked blurry when I was preaching. Other lenses allowed me to see clearly all the way to the back of the balcony, but I could not read anything right in front of my face. And so I went to an eye doctor and got some new contact lenses. At first they worked wonderfully. I could see at a distance. I could see right in front of me. I could read—even a menu in a dark restaurant. It was great! And then one morning after I put the lenses in, I felt off balance all day. I thought, *These lenses are worse than the other ones.* I kept running into walls. I would turn a corner and run into the door. Everything was blurry, and I had a terrible headache. As I was driving home, I thought, *These people are driving crazy on the road today; why are they honking at me?* And then when I got home, I drove into the garage and scraped the side mirror on the garage door. So I went back to the eye doctor.

"These new lenses you gave me aren't working at all!" I said.

She very patiently tested my eyes again, then said, "It's always helpful if you put the lens meant for your right eye in your right eye, and the one meant for your left eye in your left eye."

Looking Through the Right Lens

It's amazing what the right lenses can do. What a difference it makes when you can see with clarity! A lot of us struggle with vision. We struggle with seeing beyond what is right in front of us because of what life throws our way—the tough times, the moments of despair. Those are the things that cloud our vision and keep us from seeing the full picture. How are we supposed to see the fullness of God's purpose and God's plan when we are dealing with something that is right in front of our faces, something that is taking all of our energy and hope?

When you are dealing with a situation, it is intensely personal. It doesn't matter what it is; it doesn't matter what age you are. If it is upsetting to you, it is intensely personal. And it clouds your vision. It keeps you from seeing the fullness of the picture.

For example, when teenagers struggle with an issue, they may think to themselves, *This is the worst day of my life. It couldn't get any worse than today.* And that feeling is entirely real for them in that moment. But if they can get perspective and be able to see beyond what they are dealing with, they begin to understand that there is a whole world out there beyond their present situation. Sometimes as parents and grandparents, we laugh to ourselves when teenagers are dealing with some issue, because we think they need to understand that this is not the worst day of their lives. But when they are in the midst of the situation, they can't get perspective. They may think that their lives are over and there is no hope.

Of course, as adults we deal with this too. Confronted with an ordeal, we wonder: *How am I going to get through this? What's going to happen?* We know our vision has been clouded, but it's still hard to see beyond the present. Could it be that we get so caught up in the despair of the world and our own suffering that we fail to remember we are citizens of hope who have a reason to rejoice, a reason to hope?

(Mary Brooke) Several years ago I was honored to be asked by friends to attend their naturalization ceremonies as they became citizens of the United States of America. I sat beside them in a room filled with several hundred people. Part of the ceremony included a "call of countries." People from many different nations stood up as their native country was called; several wore the traditional dress of their country of origin.

As the judge administered the oath of allegiance for naturalized American citizens, this diverse group of people, of all ages and colors, stood up, raised their right hands, and took the oath. When the judge proclaimed that they were now naturalized American citizens, every person in the room cheered and applauded. Some laughed, some cried, some hugged friends and family, some waved small American flags. It was a moving, memorable event, and I was blessed to be a part of it and share the joyous occasion with my friends.

My friends fled their country of origin because of religious persecution. They came to America and began a new life, grateful for the freedom to practice their Christian beliefs. As I looked around the room at the new American citizens, I wished I could hear all of their stories. Why had they left the countries of their birth and sought a new home in a new country? What would it be like to take off the lens of citizenship of one nation and put on the lens of American citizenship? More important,

Could it be that
we get so caught up
in the despair of the
world and our own
suffering that we fail
to remember we are
citizens of hope
who have a reason
to rejoice,
a reason to hope?

what vision of a new life did they have, and how did they move forward in hope to achieve it? That's an important question for all who would desire to become citizens of hope.

Everyone looks at life through some kind of lens. For some it's a political lens; for others, an economic lens. There are lots of different ways we look at life. But the lens that makes the most sense for us as Christians is the story of Jesus. It's the story of God's love poured out for us through Jesus. When we put on the lens of the life, death, and resurrection of Jesus Christ, everything begins to grow clearer. The clarity of our vision is enhanced when we choose to look at life through that lens. We can see things in a different way than if we're just viewing life through our own personal lens.

In Paul's letter to the Romans, the fifth chapter provides us with pivotal, foundational verses, giving us a picture of what looking at life through the lens of the life, death and resurrection of Jesus can mean for our lives in terms of helping us become citizens of hope:

Therefore, since we have been declared righteous by faith, we have peace with God through our Lord Jesus Christ, through whom we have also obtained access by faith into this grace in which we stand, and we rejoice in the hope of God's glory. Not only this, but we also rejoice in sufferings, knowing that suffering produces endurance, and endurance, character, and character, hope. And hope does not disappoint, because the love of God has been poured out in our hearts through the Holy Spirit who was given to us.
(Romans 5:1-5 NET)

Source of Hope

When we look at life through the lens of the life, death, and resurrection of Jesus Christ, we learn this first: we have a source of hope. This source of hope is beyond our own strength, beyond what we can do, beyond what we can muster up from our own personal courage. Many of us like to think of ourselves as positive thinkers. Positive thinking is based on the positive thinker's ability to think positively. It means you have to work at it; and if you are having a bad day, or a bad year, or a bad decade, that's very tough.

Hope is different than positive thinking because hope is grounded in God's love. Hope is God's gift to us. Paul tells us that we have this source of hope beyond our own ability. It's what God has done for us. God has justified us; God has made us right. It's through believing, through trusting in God, that we are made right with God and have access to this grace in which we stand. We have a ground of hope. Jesus Christ has made God's love accessible to us. That's why looking at life through the lens of the story of Jesus helps my life and your life. Beyond our own human strength, our own human weakness, there is a source of hope and strength for us found in God's love. Jesus Christ has made God's love accessible to us. In Jesus Christ, God has become close and personal to each one of us. It's in his love that we begin to see things in a new way.

When people are faced with trials and tragedies, they often make comments such as, "I don't know how we're going to get through this"; "We don't know how we're going to deal with this"; "We've never been through this before."

We don't know how to get through this tough time in our marriage because we've never had tough times like these.

We don't know how we're going to deal with teenagers. We've never had teenagers.

I've never lost a job before. I've never been in this kind of economic distress.

We don't know how we are going to deal with this situation with our child because we've never had a child in distress.

We don't know how we are going to deal with this death because we've never lost a parent/spouse/child.

When we are hit with these kinds of realities, our vision is completely blurred. It's like not being able to see the forest for the trees; all we can see is this event right in front of our faces. We can't see the forest of God's possibilities and opportunities. So we cry out: "I don't know how we are going to get through this. I don't know if we can do this. I don't know if I can even keep breathing."

But with the right lens, we can begin to see what God is doing in the midst of these situations. God comes alongside us, often through other people, walking with us through those trials and tragedies.

When we allow God to use us to reach out to others, we often will hear them say: "I didn't know how we were going to get through that, but God gave us strength day by day. We look back on that time and realize God carried us through. It was the toughest time of our lives. It's still hard today, but God has been there to help us."

That's what Paul wanted the Romans to know: that there was a source of strength available to them beyond their own strength, and that they had access to that strength through the gift of Jesus Christ. We do too. Through the lens of his life, we see that there is someone there to help us during those tough times.

What is that source of hope for you? Have you ever considered that you need a source of strength and hope?

We have both spent many summer vacations in Colorado since our childhood and continuing into our adult years. Several summers ago, we met someone who was building a new home. One of the locals was talking about the people building the new house and said, "They would do well to dig their well for their water in the wintertime." When we asked why, he shared that if you dig a well in the spring or summer, the water table is higher, and if you settle for that, you might be in trouble when you go to draw water in the wintertime, when the water table is lower. But if you dig a well in the winter, you'll have no trouble year-round.

That is wisdom not just for building a home, but also for building a life. Do you have a source of hope that is deep enough to continuously offer you living hope? Paul reminds us that it is through Christ that we have access to the grace of God and that is the foundation upon which we stand. Putting your faith in Christ is like digging your well in the wintertime, offering you hope in good times and in difficulty. It is a source you can count on!

Suffering Does Not Have the Last Word

The second thing that Paul suggests to us is that suffering does not have the last word. When we put on our "Jesus lenses" and look at life through the life, death, and resurrection of Jesus Christ, we see that suffering does not have the last word. Paul says we even rejoice in our sufferings because we know this—that we Christians can find joy in the midst of our suffering because we know that suffering produces endurance, and endurance produces character, and character produces hope (see Romans 5:3-4). Suffering is not the last word in that sentence, and suffering does *not* have the last word.

One of the most important decisions we make in life is what we do when we suffer. When you find yourself in distress, when circumstances have gone against you, when you are in a physical battle for your health or dealing with spiritual anguish, what do you do and where do you turn in those moments? That story is played out so many times in Scripture. God hears the cries of people suffering, and God offers help and hope to those who are hurting. As Psalm 30:5 says, "Weeping may linger for the night, / but joy comes with the morning." All suffering is temporary; it will not last, and you do not have to wallow in it or stay in it. This is where having good vision for your life makes all the difference, and why the lens of the story of Jesus can make such a difference in our lives. We can see clearly that because of what God has done in the life, death, and resurrection of Jesus, suffering will give way to hope. And, along the way, God gives us endurance and helps build our character. That character building leads us to greater clarity in our vision.

(Clayton) When I was in high school, I played football and basketball. My dad was the pastor of a large church and was very busy, and I don't know how he did it, but he managed to be at almost all of the events involving his four children. His presence was a powerful example, something I admired about him.

As is the case with sports, our team didn't win every game. I'd come home from the game, my dad would come into my room, and we'd sit there and replay the game—what happened, what should have happened. And after those losses, I could always predict what he would say every time: "Well, you know it builds character."

I'd think, *Really? That's your word of wisdom?* (When you're a teenager, what does your dad know, right?) As it turns out, he knew a lot, and of course he was right. But at the time, with my youthful perspective, my thought was, *I don't care about character—I just want to win! I'm sick and tired of losing!*

One of the reasons Mary Brooke and I both love to watch sports so much is that so many life lessons are offered to us through sports. It's more than just the winning and losing—learning to strive to be your best, working together with others toward a common goal, sacrificing, believing, enduring—all of it plays out in our lives.

When we put on our
"Jesus lenses" and
look at life through
the life, death,
and resurrection
of Jesus Christ,
we see that suffering
does not have
the last word.

A friend of mine, who is a college football coach, loves to preach to his team about adversity. He says that in every game things go wrong, and adversity is part of the game. He tells his team that it's not about making mistakes; it's about what we do when we make mistakes—what we do when things go against our team. His belief is that adversity doesn't shape character; it reveals character. We have to know and believe that when things go wrong, the game is not over. The team that wins is not always the team that makes the fewest mistakes—it's usually the team that responds in a positive way and keeps playing the game after mistakes are made.

In Romans 5, Paul says that when we suffer, we do so with an alert expectation that suffering is not the last word in our story. Suffering builds endurance and perseverance. And in building perseverance and endurance, character is forged and revealed. Each of us goes through situations in which our character is being built, shaped, and revealed through adversity. And during those times we often wonder, *Is this ever going to end in a good way?*

The good news is that, yes, it does! When we view our lives through the life, death, and resurrection of Jesus, we see that it's a story that didn't end on a cross or in a tomb—it ended in the hope of resurrection. That's why the story of Jesus is *the* story—the lens that helps us see that even in our sufferings, suffering is not the final word. Ours is a story that ends in hope.

(Mary Brooke) When our father was dying, his last month on this earth was not an easy one. He was in the

ICU in the hospital for three weeks before he was moved to palliative care. And he was suffering. Day after day I would go to the hospital with my family and sometimes spend the night, and we were all exhausted. On one of those days of just utter despair, Clayton felt moved to do something. There was a dry erase board in the room, as there often is in a hospital room, which displayed the nurse's name, the date, the goal for the day. Clayton wiped that board clean and wrote four words that he and our father had often talked about: suffering, endurance, character—and then in bold letters, the one word Clayton wanted him to see above all else—HOPE.

Hope. This is how the story ends. Suffering will not have the last word for you or for me. Ours is a story that, through the lens of Jesus Christ, ends in hope.

Hope Never Fails Us

Paul tells us that hope never fails us. It never disappoints us or leaves us lacking. Why does hope never fail us? Because God's love has been poured into our hearts through the Holy Spirit. God continues to love us and never abandons us. That's the good news.

(Clayton) Several years ago my wife and I decided to do some landscaping in our backyard. The plan included relocating a banana plant from one part of the yard to another. We had watched this banana plant, and it was resilient. Every year we cut it back to almost nothing and would watch it grow back six or seven feet tall. But transplanting it was different. I would go out to water it, and it was just a little brown nub. This went on for weeks with no sign of life. Lori told me on several occasions she thought it was dead. The hot Texas summer we had that year didn't help matters. After months of watering and hoping that brown nub would do something, I began to lose hope. The banana plant was a goner. And then one evening in the late summer I went out to water some other plants. I walked by the brown nub that had been the banana plant, and the smallest green sprig was sticking up in the middle of it. It was alive! All those months we had kept watering and hoping, and about the time we were ready to give up, new life sprung forth! By the fall it was full grown, and a beautiful reminder to us: Keep on watering. You never know what might happen.

A lot of things in life fail; a lot of things in life don't go right. But God's love keeps pouring into our hearts, watering our souls, trying to give us a picture of hope, trying to help us know that there is hope for us in every situation—that despair and the suffering of this world will not have the last word.

Where does hope come from? Where does the hope come for you and me in our lives and in our struggles? God pours love into our hearts. That is the ground of our hope. That is why we are citizens of hope and not citizens of despair. That is why in the midst of our sufferings we can look with alert expectation to what God is doing.

God is still God, and God is still love. God's love is continuously poured into our hearts through God's Holy Spirit. May God grant us the eyes to see that the ground of our hope is in the story of Jesus, whose life, death, and resurrection give us an unchanging framework through which we see hope. And hope never fails us. That is a bedrock belief for citizens of hope!

Thank you, merciful God, for always pouring love into my heart. Forgive me for those times I have lost perspective on my life due to my own poor vision. Give me your vision to be able to see that because of the life, death, and resurrection of Jesus, there is always hope. Thank you for sending Jesus to make your grace accessible to me and to the world. Remind me today that suffering never has the last word. You have promised that suffering will teach me to endure, that learning to endure will build my character, and that character will reveal hope to me along the way. Help me to live as a citizen of hope. And Lord, if there is someone I meet along the way who is suffering, give me the courage to offer a word of support and hope. Guide me, O Lord, with your holy vision. I pray this in Jesus' name. Amen.

 **REFLECT**

⚓ Port of Entry

Reread Romans 5:1-5 (see page 42).

In Romans 5:1-5, Paul begins to tell us about the fruits and benefits of this justification. Our faith in Christ gives us peace and assurance, the knowledge that God's saving grace has been made accessible to all of us through Jesus Christ. God's grace gives us a foundation on which to stand and is the basis for hope in every situation. Even in our times of suffering, we can be confident that suffering is not the last word. Suffering produces endurance, and endurance produces character, and character produces hope, and hope never fails us. Even when we are suffering, God's love is being poured into our hearts through the Holy Spirit—God's way of reminding us that suffering will never be the last word.

Have you ever been through a "character-building" hardship and felt there was no way out? What happened?

How did God help you work through that situation?

 Customs Declaration Form

---

What insights did you gain from each section in this chapter?

Looking Through the Right Lens

Source of Hope

God

Suffering Does Not Have the Last Word

Hope Never Fails Us

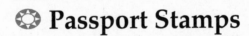

✪ Passport Stamps

What is "stamped" on your heart that you will remember most from this chapter?

Trust God!
Trust Jesus!

CHAPTER 3

FED BY HOPE

For I received from the Lord what I also handed on to you,
that the Lord Jesus on the night when he was betrayed took
a loaf of bread, and when he had given thanks, he broke
it and said, "This is my body that is for you. Do this in
remembrance of me." In the same way he took the cup also,
after supper, saying, "This cup is the new covenant in my
blood. Do this, as often as you drink it, in remembrance of
me." For as often as you eat this bread and drink the cup,
you proclaim the Lord's death until he comes.

(1 Corinthians 11:23-26)

CHAPTER 3

FED BY HOPE

Where does a citizen of hope go to be fed? A car needs fuel, or at least some energy source, in order to keep running. What is it that keeps us going as Christians? What provides the fuel that empowers us to stay strong in our identity and find hope on a daily basis?

(Clayton) When you live in Texas, you end up eating a lot of barbecue. Everyone seems to have a favorite barbecue restaurant, and each will argue that it's the sauce, the meat, the smoker on which it is cooked, and the people who cook it that make all the difference. But my favorite barbecue place is really about the experience as well as the sauce and all the rest. It's a hole-in-the-wall restaurant, really just an old shack in the middle of Dallas. There's not much seating, so the crowd often spills over into the outdoors, and what little seating is available is comprised of benches with old school desktops attached. Not much has changed in the décor over the last thirty years or so, and the smoky barbecue smell permeates the entire building.

When you order, they call you by initial: "C.O., your order is ready!" "M.B.C., your order is ready!" People of all walks of life enter those doors: construction workers, workers from the nearby hospital district, businessmen and women, people from the nearby Salvation Army Center—it's a melting pot of people of all colors and cultures coming together to be fed. And they will be well fed. It has always reminded me of what the church of Jesus Christ could and should be.

What Feeds You?

So where do you go to be fed? Have you ever really thought about what feeds you? Where do you really find help, hope, and the strength that sustains you? We need food to stay alive. Instinctively we know this—from our earliest moments of life we cry out for food when we are hungry. In a similar way, we have a spiritual hunger, and instinctively we know we have this need for something more. The problem is that much of what is offered to us as filling only leaves us empty.

(Mary Brooke) Years ago my husband, Vic, made an important observation of what it means to be fed by hope in describing the difference between an epicurean table and a eucharistic table. The term *epicurean* comes from the Greek philosopher Epicurus and is used to describe those devoted to the enjoyment of fine food and drink. The term *Eucharist* means "thanksgiving" and is used to describe the sacrament of Holy Communion.

While we were visiting my parents, Vic was reading through the magazines they subscribed to, and he noted that there were several epicurean magazines, those publications devoted entirely to food and drink. Most of these magazines were gift subscriptions, he learned, and while my mother enjoyed reading them, she rarely tried any of the recipes. She usually prepared the dishes she had been making for years, the "family favorites" that were in demand. She would spend hours in the kitchen, cooking and baking, each dish a gift of love.

But the difference that Vic saw at a eucharistic table was not only the delicious food but also the generous helpings of love and thanksgiving. The meal event itself was a feast of fellowship with one another, recognition of the Christ present with us. We left the table filled with nourishment of both body and soul. A eucharistic table is indeed a glimpse of the "heavenly banquet"[1] being prepared for us.

We all, no doubt, remember times when we dined on dishes that were exquisite. But epicurean tables, while momentarily delightful, can never fully satisfy us. Only the Eucharist meal can do that.

How easy it is for us to buy into what our culture says will ultimately feed us! Advertisements constantly bombard us with messages that we will find what we have been looking for if we buy their "stuff." So we buy the stuff and the longing remains because it never really satisfies what our hungry hearts are searching for. The longing remains and we keep on buying more stuff, thinking somehow this will be the fix, the cure. Subconsciously we tell ourselves, *I'll be happy if I have this product or that thing; I'll be satisfied if I have this position; all my problems go away if only I could make $10,000, $25,000, or $100,000 more than I do now!* And we find ourselves, with or without all of those things, still hungry for something more.

Something More

That something more we are longing for is found in our relationship with God through Jesus Christ. You and I were born to be citizens of hope, and we find this hope—this sustaining food for our lives—through a relationship with Christ.

How does that relationship become real to us so that we can experience this life-giving food? Throughout the centuries, Christians have found that when they feast on the body and blood of Christ, something mystical and mysterious happens. It is in celebrating Holy Communion as a means of God's grace that we are fed in ways that nothing on this earth can do for us. From the earliest days of the church, disciples and followers of Jesus have gathered around tables, and when they broke the bread, they experienced the living Christ present with them, giving them hope to face any situation in life they came up against. Through the holy mystery called Holy Communion, we are fed with an incredible hope.

(Clayton) A little boy came up to me before worship one Sunday and said, "Pastor Clayton, is this one of the Sundays when we get snacks?"

I knelt down to talk to him and said, "Yes! Today is a Communion Sunday, and you get a piece of bread and grape juice." And I should have added, "...and so much more!"

Many Christians look at Holy Communion as a ritual they go through every Sunday, once a month, or even occasionally, and they never really consider its meaning. Rather than going through the motions and getting our "Sunday snack," what if we learned to fully participate in this holy mystery in which Christ is made real to us? We might just find that there is "something more" that feeds our souls as nothing else can do.

In the Communion liturgy of our church, we talk about the great mystery of the Christian faith: "Christ has died; Christ is risen; Christ will come again."[2] Have you ever wondered what these words are all about? They are, in some ways, a mystery to be discovered and experienced. What can these words mean in terms of helping us understand what we are experiencing in the Lord's Supper? What might they mean for our lives on a practical level?

Christ Has Died

As we gather around the Lord's Table and receive the body of Christ, we remember the self-sacrifice of Jesus Christ. God so loved the world that God gave his Son, and in his suffering and death, we find life and salvation from our sins. Jesus' suffering on the cross connects with our suffering in the world today.

Have you ever felt alone? Have you ever experienced a situation in life when you felt hopeless, as though you were abandoned? On the cross Jesus experienced all of that and more. One of the pivotal moments in the gospel story is when Jesus cries out from the cross, "My God, my God, why have you forsaken me?" (Mark 15:34). In this moment in time, Jesus, both fully human and fully divine, experiences the fullness of human emptiness and brokenness, and divinely participates in it. This is the defining moment when God fully understands the depth of human misery, and humans begin to understand the depth to which God's love will go to reach us in our brokenness.

If you have ever suffered, if life has ever handed you more than you could ever bear, this is the story that connects us to a God who suffers with us and for us. Not content to remain at a distance, God has become intimately acquainted with our hurts, our sins, and our fears, through the death of Jesus on the cross.

(Mary Brooke) Rearing two teenage sons was the hardest experience of my life! I learned what it meant to "pray without ceasing" (1 Thessalonians 5:17) because there were so many times, day and night, when I had no place to go but God. In those gut-wrenching, honest prayers in which I wrestled with God, questioning and crying out in despair, I would often hear God speak, not with an answer but with a question: "How do you think I feel about what happened to my Son?"

Over time, I began to realize that the entire narrative of Jesus' life and death addresses every human hurt and circumstance. Knowing that God had also wept like a heartbroken parent for a child, knowing that Jesus had suffered the unimaginable, helped me feel God's understanding and caring. God was with me, and that gave me hope that together, we would come through this.

Why do we recall the death of Jesus when we gather for this meal? Because we remember that in our own death, our own suffering, we have One who has come to be with us, who identifies with us, who has experienced everything that we have experienced, or ever will experience. We are not alone in those moments.

Whenever you are hurting, remember that Christ suffers with you. You are not alone. God so loved the world that God gave God's Son for all who hurt, for all who suffer, for all who die, that we may know that we are in this with Christ and Christ is in this with us. We are fed by this hope that we are not alone.

71

Christ Is Risen

The second thing we remember in this holy mystery is that Christ is risen. We remember the death of Jesus, but we also remember that God raised him up. So in the Communion meal, we have this tangible physical reminder: this body was broken, this blood was shed, but God was not finished. God is not content to let suffering and death have the last word.

That is why we can never give up. That is why we never say it is hopeless. This meal reminds us that God is not through with any of our lives, that God is a God of resurrection and new life.

A great story is told about what happened during a church finance committee meeting. The finance committee chair prayed a beautiful prayer at the beginning of the meeting: "Lord, we know that with you all things are possible, and we ask that you be with us as we deliberate on the finances of our church." Then, as the finances of the church were reviewed and the meeting came to a close, he said, "Ladies and gentlemen, the financial situation of this church is completely hopeless. I don't know what we're going to do."

The finance committee chair needed to remind himself of his opening prayer! With God, nothing is impossible. That is the word for us. But so often in our lives we become citizens of despair. We become people whose nationality becomes hopelessness, doom, and gloom. We look around the world and think there is no hope.

Indeed, there are countless situations happening around the world that are so mind-boggling that we think: how will the world go on?

In our own personal lives, we face times when we are just absolutely broken by life. We think, "There is no future for me, no hope for me, and no hope for this situation that I'm facing." But in this meal, this holy mystery that we celebrate, we are brought back to our true nationality. This meal tells us that we are citizens of hope. We feast on this hope of resurrection, this God whose love never gives up, this God whose love never fails. This meal reminds us of our primary citizenship as a nation of hope. We are citizens of hope.

Each time you receive Holy Communion, remember that no matter your situation and no matter what is happening in our world today, God is a God of resurrection. As the Scriptures proclaim, the same God who raised up his Son, Jesus Christ, will also raise us up. It's God's promise. And it's not just after we die—it's here and now. God is at work resurrecting and bringing new life and hope to you and me.

This resurrection power helps us find healing from the brokenness of our own lives and our relationships. It has the power to tear down the walls that separate us from others. United in this Spirit of the resurrected Christ, we find the capacity to live out our calling to be his body in the world. Our connection to the living Christ even helps us reconcile in love with people, even when we disagree with them.

(Mary Brooke) Have you ever encountered a fellow Christian with whom you disagreed about almost everything? I have! I was once in a Sunday school class that included such a person. He was very intelligent, very likable, a devoted family man, and a lifelong member of this particular church where my husband was serving as pastor; but he and I had very different worldviews. It seemed that in every Sunday school class and Bible study we were in, we argued on different sides of the issues. I found myself approaching Sunday school as a sparring match instead of a community of believers eager to learn and grow in their faith!

One Sunday, following such a debate, I was feeling particularly frustrated. The worship service that morning included the celebration of Holy Communion. As I knelt at the Communion rail to receive the elements, I noticed that this man was kneeling right beside me. Seeing the bread and chalice, and hearing the words, "This is my body, broken for you; this is my blood, shed for you," helped me receive a new insight. It was as if Jesus was whispering to me about the man kneeling next to me: "He is my child too. I died for him too. I love him as much as I love you."

As we rose from the Communion rail, I smiled at him. He smiled back and we embraced. Although we continued to voice our different opinions in the classes we attended, I felt different about him. He was my brother in Christ! We could appreciate and respect each other, despite our differences.

We remained friends over many years and stayed in touch. When he died, my husband spoke at his funeral, standing next to that same Communion rail where my friend and I had knelt all those years before.

The invitation to Holy Communion is issued by Christ our Lord, who "invites to his table all who love him, who earnestly repent of their sin and seek to live in peace with one another."[3] These poignant words remind us that Christ's sacrifice was made for all his children, and we must seek forgiveness and reconciliation with others in order to be fed by the Bread of Life.

Communion is a sign that the risen Christ unites all his followers into one body, the body of Christ.

Christ Will Come Again

The third aspect of the mystery of the Christian faith referred to in the Communion liturgy is that Christ will come again. In this Communion meal, we are pointing forward to God's ultimate victory. It is a statement of hope, reminding us that this is God's world. The God who raised his Son from the dead is not content to leave us alone and abandoned, without hope. God's promise is that this same Jesus who died and rose again will come in final judgment as the fulfillment of history. As we experience Holy Communion, we are given sustenance, fed by this hope. It is, as the hymn writer suggested, a "foretaste of glory divine."[4] God's ultimate victory is not just *someday* at the close of the age; God's at work *today* bringing about that victory.

Communion is
a sign that the
risen Christ unites
all his followers
into one body,
the body of Christ.

(Clayton) Several years ago our church did an informal survey about worship. One of the questions asked was, "When in worship do you feel closest to Christ?" There were many different responses. For some, it was the music, the hymn singing and the special music from our choirs. For others, it was during the prayer time, or during the Scripture reading or sermon. But a very large number of people said it was when they received Holy Communion, the Lord's Supper. One of the comments shared by a member said it so well: "When I kneel down and the bread and cup are shared, I know that God is with me and that, if God is with me, I can face whatever."

"Christ has died; Christ is risen; Christ will come again."[5] When we think of that whole statement, that mystery, that Christ will come again, we understand that God is at work to bring things around, to set things right. God is at work in the world today in ways that we can't even begin to imagine, to set things right, to bring justice to this world. It's already happening. And in this meal we are pointing forward to what is already true—that we feast at this heavenly banquet, that we have this foretaste of what is real, what is going to happen, that God's love will win. Sometimes that is all we need to know: God's love will win.

Each time you partake of the sacrament of Holy Communion, it's an invitation to renew your citizenship. We are citizens of hope! It's a hope that is fed to us in this holy meal. And it satisfies like nothing in this world can satisfy.

"When I kneel down
and the bread
and cup are shared,
I know that God is
with me and that,
if God is with me,
I can face whatever."

You can't buy it, you can't spend your way to it, you can't swipe your card to it, you can't get it through technology. It is God's gift poured out for you, the hope of the world in Jesus Christ. When the life, death, and resurrection of Jesus Christ become our frame of reference, everything changes. The whole landscape of our world changes because we can look out and see that in the seemingly hopeless situations of our world, God is not finished. God is not finished with any of us. God is not finished with this world. God is at work through the death, the resurrection, and the promise of Christ's return to bring us hope right now.

(Clayton) When we were young children, our father had a hobby—beekeeping! He had three beehives in the backyard, and he enjoyed having honey that was produced by the bees in his own backyard. But when we came along and started to play out in the backyard, he knew he needed to find a new home for the bees. (We've always suspected our mother may have had input on that decision.)

Our father knew a man in the church who had beehives and offered to give him our hives. One Saturday the man showed up at the parsonage, loaded the three hives onto his pickup truck, and took them away. The next morning our father was serving the Lord's Supper to his congregation. As he went down the chancel rail, he arrived in front of a man who stuck two extremely swollen hands up to receive the bread. My father looked up into the badly swollen face of the man who had taken the bees the previous day. After worship, he found the man and asked, "What happened?" The man shared that as he was unloading the hives he dropped one and was immediately swarmed and stung all over by the bees. My father asked, "Why in the world would you come to church this morning with all those stings and with your face so swollen?" He replied, "I thought about not coming, but it's Communion Sunday. I never miss Communion Sunday. It's too important."

Yes, it is important. The living God meets us in the breaking of the bread and the sharing of the cup. We should never miss an opportunity to partake of this sacred meal. It begins when we respond to the invitation to come to the table. It's more than just the bread and cup; it's the experience. In this holy mystery, in the breaking of the bread and the drinking of the cup, our lives are being transformed by Jesus Christ, the hope of the world. As citizens of hope, this is the meal that feeds our souls.

Loving and giving God, only you can satisfy my hungry heart. Too often I have tried to fill that longing with other things. Thank you for offering your grace to me and to all the world. When I receive the Lord's Supper, help me to focus on your promises. Christ has died, suffering with and for me and forgiving my sins. Christ is risen, offering me new life and new hope. Christ will come again, reminding me that God's love will ultimately triumph over all. Give me the faith to believe that today and the strength to live it. Send me forth to invite others to come to the holy table of grace and taste for themselves the bread of life, the source of our hope, Jesus the Christ. In his name I pray. Amen.

REFLECT

⚓ Port of Entry

Reread 1 Corinthians 11:23-26 (see page 64).

Paul reminds the church about the actions and words of Jesus on that night when he was betrayed. He took a loaf of bread, gave thanks, broke it, and said, "'This is my body that is for you. Do this in remembrance of me.' In the same way he took the cup also, after supper, saying, 'This cup is the new covenant in my blood. Do this, as often as you drink it, in remembrance of me'" (1 Corinthians 11:24-25). Paul says that when we partake of the Lord's Supper in this way, we are "proclaiming the Lord's death until he comes" (v. 26). This is the holy mystery: Christ has died; Christ is risen; Christ will come again. The story is always pointing us toward hope—Christ will ultimately triumph, and his reign will be on earth as it is in heaven. When we celebrate the Lord's Supper and remember his words, we are anticipating that future hope even as we claim the presence of Christ in the midst of our current reality.

Has there been a time when receiving Holy Communion took on a special meaning for you? If so, what made it special or gave it special meaning?

✍ Customs Declaration Form

What insights did you gain from each section in this chapter?

What Feeds You?

Something More

Christ Has Died

Christ Is Risen

Christ Will Come Again

☼ Passport Stamps

What is "stamped" on your heart that you will remember most from this chapter?

To appreciate communion for it's true purpose. Even tho I knew it's purpose, I will now try to always think of Jesus' suffering, then rising when taking communion

CHAPTER 4

SECOND LINE LIVING

Jesus said to her, "I am the resurrection and the life. Those who believe in me, even though they die, will live, and everyone who lives and believes in me will never die. Do you believe this?"

(John 11:25-26)

But Mary stood weeping outside the tomb. As she wept, she bent over to look into the tomb; and she saw two angels in white, sitting where the body of Jesus had been lying, one at the head and the other at the feet. They said to her, "Woman, why are you weeping?" She said to them, "They have taken away my Lord, and I do not know where they have laid him." When she had said this, she turned around and saw Jesus standing there, but she did not know that it was Jesus. Jesus said to her, "Woman, why are you weeping? Whom are you looking for?" Supposing him to be the gardener, she said to him, "Sir, if you have carried him away, tell me where you have laid him, and I will take him away." Jesus said to her, "Mary!" She turned and said to him in Hebrew, "Rabbouni!" (which means Teacher). Jesus said to her, "Do not hold on to me, because I have not yet ascended to the Father. But go to my brothers and say to them, 'I am ascending to my Father and your Father, to my God and your God.'" Mary Magdalene went and announced to the disciples, "I have seen the Lord"; and she told them that he had said these things to her.

(John 20:11-18)

CHAPTER 4

SECOND LINE LIVING

Jesus said, "I am the resurrection and the life. Those who believe in me even though they die, will live, and everyone who lives and believes in me shall never die" (John 11:25-26).

Do you ever have days when it's hard to believe that? Days of such heartache and tragedy that the good news of resurrection fails to reach you? We don't always hear that word; we can't always believe that word.

One tradition that exemplifies the power of Jesus' resurrection comes from our home state of Louisiana. The tradition of the second line originated in New Orleans, dating back to the early 1800s when slaves and free people of color created what are known as "jazz funerals." In these funerals, the "first line" is made up of the family, walking slowly and mournfully to the cemetery. But when the burial is over, the "second line," composed of a jazz band and friends, begin parading through the streets, joyfully dancing and celebrating the life of the deceased, and helping release his or her soul. Leading the family out of the cemetery, out of a place of death and sorrow, the second line joyously proclaims:

> *Oh, when the saints go marching in . . .*
> *O Lord, I want to be in that number*
> *When the saints go marching in*[1]

Just a few months after our younger brother died of brain cancer, and a year and a half after our father's death, our mother died quite unexpectedly in her sleep. She just went to sleep and never woke up.

The day of our mother's funeral was one of the hardest days of our lives. The conclusion of her memorial service was the same as at the services for our father and brother—a lone bagpiper processed down the aisle of the church playing "The Lord's My Shepherd." When he reached the front pew where our family was seated, he turned and led us out to a traditional Scottish tune, "Will Ye No Come Back Again?" These words, written by our ancestor, Scottish poet Carolina Oliphant (Lady Nairne), are about Bonnie Prince Charles leaving Scotland. With its slow and mournful tune, it is considered the Scottish farewell. Written in a Scottish brogue, the chorus poignantly asks:

Will ye no' come back again?
Will ye no' come back again?
Better lo'ed ye canna be;
Will ye no' come back again?[2]

Our mother's service was held during Mardi Gras, on "Fat Tuesday," the day before Ash Wednesday. To pay tribute to her Louisiana heritage, we decided that we needed a "second line." After the family had been led out of the sanctuary by the bagpiper and reached the fellowship hall, a jazz band in the back of the sanctuary began to play "When the Saints Go Marching In." Friends who comprised the second line led the congregation into the fellowship hall with lively steps, waving their handkerchiefs. And our mourning was turned to dancing!

Living the Resurrection Faith

The second line makes all the difference. The tradition of the second line is that while the mourners are still dealing with the reality of death, when the funeral dirge is still playing in their ears, the second line fires up the song of resurrection, the song of hope, the song of new life. God's gift to us is resurrection and life. As the mourners are walking away from the grave, they begin to hear that joyful sound and to know that hope is on the way. New life is coming.

Resurrection is not just a concept; it is a reality. It's a reality claimed by Christians because of this story that was told long ago about a woman who went to the tomb.

Mary Magdalene, whose life had been in such darkness before she met Jesus, watched along with Jesus' disciples as he was taken, arrested, beaten, and crucified. They watched him die. They saw him laid in a tomb that was covered by a large stone.

But early on the first day of the week, while it was still dark, Mary and a few others went to the tomb, and there they found the stone rolled away and the tomb empty. When Mary came out of that tomb in bewilderment, all she could hear was the funeral dirge, the music of the first line. Through her tears she couldn't see any reality of resurrection. All she could see was the reality of death. "Where have they taken my Lord's body? I saw him die." And then she heard her name, "Mary, Mary." She looked up through her tears, and she could see it was Jesus. He called her by name: "Mary." She heard that second line music begin to play as she looked at Jesus and saw her Lord lifted up, her Lord alive and raised from the dead by the power of God.

Resurrection changes everything. Jesus said, "I am the resurrection and the life" (John 11:25). Jesus is a window into the nature of who God is. God's very nature, the ground of being in which we stand today, is the very hope of resurrection. It's at the heart of who God is: resurrection and new life. Even as we hear the mournful music still playing in our ears, God is firing up the second line, firing up the resurrection music, letting us know that death cannot win.

Resurrection is not
just a concept;
it is a reality.
Resurrection changes
everything.

(Mary Brooke) My husband, Vic, and I spent an entire week with our son, daughter-in-law, and two grandsons, awaiting the birth of our third grandchild. Tests were unable to conclusively determine the baby's gender, so we eagerly looked forward to finding out the "old-fashioned way."

The due date came and went, and with each passing day, I grew more anxious. Vic was scheduled to preach his first sermon at a new church appointment. Would we have to leave before the baby was born? We'd had the joy and privilege of being at the hospital for both of our grandsons' births and certainly didn't want to miss this one. I sent up fervent prayers to God the night before our absolute deadline for departure.

Awaking about six o'clock the next morning, I remembered my father's death at this time, on this date four years before. With sadness, I relived that event. But my quiet reverie was interrupted by my son and daughter-in-law—she was in labor, and they were leaving for the hospital!

Vic and I cared for our grandsons and took them to the hospital, where our daughter-in-law's parents and brother joined us to await the birth. About half past noon, our son appeared in the doorway of the waiting room, smiled, and motioned us to follow him. I took my two grandsons by the hand and walked down the hall. We peered around the door to see my daughter-in-law holding a tiny bundle with a pink cap! After three brothers, two sons, and two grandsons, all of whom I loved dearly, I had been blessed with a granddaughter!

I felt a "resurrection moment" as I recalled standing beside my father's bedside four years to the day as he breathed his last breath, and now I rejoiced beside the bedside of a little one breathing her first breath, the next generation of our family.

My granddaughter's birthday, which is also the anniversary of my father's death, has become a powerful symbol for me of our resurrection faith.

Faith Overcomes Fear

Because of the second line music of resurrection, faith overcomes fear. It is our faith in God that helps us overcome our fears in life. Every one of us has experienced fear. Some of us are afraid of death, some of us are afraid of life, some of us are afraid of failing, some of us are afraid of succeeding beyond our wildest dreams, some of us are afraid of financial situations, some of us are afraid of health situations.

All through the Bible you read stories about people being afraid. Even those closest to Jesus, such as Peter and Mary Magdalene, had moments when they were afraid. And each time, Jesus said to them, "Do not be afraid" (see Matthew 14:27; 28:10). Those early disciples give us one of the greatest proofs that resurrection is real. These disciples were so fearful when Jesus was arrested and crucified that they either denied they knew Jesus, hid in fear, or stayed at a distance to protect themselves. After their encounter with the risen Christ, however, their faith helped them to place their fear in the proper perspective. Peter, the same one who denied he knew Jesus, just weeks later would stand before the very people who crucified Jesus and proclaim Jesus as the Messiah. We can learn to deal with our fears when we learn to trust in the God of resurrection and new life. Our faith in Christ gives us the foundation to face our fears.

Fear gets in the way of our living. God calls us to have resurrection faith. When the funeral dirge music of fear begins to grip our lives, we need to listen for the second line music of resurrection. That's when the hallelujahs begin to ring in our ears. That's when we hear that second line singing: "faith overcomes fear." The prophet Isaiah said,

> But those who wait for the LORD shall renew their
> strength,
>   they shall mount up with wings like eagles,
> they shall run and not be weary,
>   they shall walk and not faint.
>
> (Isaiah 40:31)

Resurrection faith overcomes all of our worldly fears.

Our father's older brother, John, was a fighter pilot stationed in England during World War II. On June 8, 1944, his plane was shot down over France. Two weeks later, our grandmother, who lived in Shreveport, Louisiana, received word that her son was missing in action. Our father, Ben, had just begun his studies at Duke Divinity School in North Carolina. He wrote the following letter to his mother:

June 22, 1944

My dearest mother,

There is very little that I can say because you already know what is in my heart. Last night after your call I thought and prayed a great deal of the night and tonight I feel strengthened and am determined to carry on in the best possible way.

I would say a few things, which I know you have already thought of and are carrying out.

Let us not give up hope. All is not lost. There are many chances that he is alive and well. I know that you will never believe, as I never shall, that he is gone until we have definite proof. Something deep inside of me tells me he is not gone. Let us keep faith with John as he would have us do. With that hope and faith let us face the long days of uncertainty and anxiety that are ahead, doing our daily tasks and work, facing the future unafraid, knowing that no matter what the outcome we can walk up to it and face it with the same courage, song in our hearts, smile on our faces, our trust in Christ, that John faced whatever came his way. Let us face this as he would have us do.

There are many more things I would like to say to you which I cannot seem to say in a letter. But your heart will tell them to you. May faith, trust and hope so fill your heart that you will become serene in spirit and be filled with the peace of God.

I love you always,
Ben

And the rest of the story? John was captured, tortured, escaped, and worked with the French underground for two months before he returned to England. He called his mother, who answered the phone, heard the voice of her son, and promptly fainted. (After all, like Mary Magdalene, the last thing you expect to experience when your heart is full of grief is resurrection and life.) John went on to live a full and remarkable life, dying just days after his ninetieth birthday. He outlived our father, his younger brother Ben, by four years.

The above letter was found in a box of old letters we discovered after the deaths of our grandmother, uncle, and father, letters they had written to one another during World War II. Letters full of faith, hope, and love.

Hope Outlasts Our Despair

Hope outlasts our despair. That's what the second line music of resurrection tells us. When we are in those funeral dirge moments of despair, depression, and darkness, when the darkness is so heavy, and so deep, we can't see our way out, God's hope, God's second line music of resurrection, begins to ring in our ears.

Mary Magdalene and the other followers of Jesus were so filled with despair that they couldn't hear the second line music of resurrection. Even when Jesus addressed her in the garden, her heart only resounded with the funeral dirge music of death. It was inconceivable to her that Jesus could be alive. Her despair was overwhelming.

Anyone who has ever grieved knows it can be like that. Life is going on all around you, but when you are grieving, you do not participate in it because your heart is not in it. That funeral dirge music is so strong it overwhelms your senses. But then there are those who come alongside you, with their second line music, the resurrection music that proclaims the good news of Jesus. Gradually, just as Mary heard Jesus call her by name, so we also begin to hear and experience God speaking a word of hope to us. Thank God for people of faith who walk with us in grief, who keep playing that resurrection song that God has raised Jesus, and because of what God has done, there is hope for our future. The despair of grief will not ultimately define our lives. Our lives will be defined by the hope and love God offers to us in the risen Christ.

We know that hope is real. With God, because of the Resurrection, there are no hopeless situations. There are no hopeless people. There is no one that is beyond resurrection and redemption. There is no one beyond the reach of God to bring new life and new hope into our lives.

Charles Wesley, along with his brother John, was the heart and soul of the Methodist movement in its early days. Charles Wesley was a great hymn writer. He wrote words of faith and set them to the bawdy barroom tunes, the secular music of his day. He set that secular music on fire by putting his words of faith to it, and people heard it as second line music of resurrection.

His hymn that is sung in churches across the globe on Easter Sunday, "Christ the Lord Is Risen Today," is a glorious song of faith. But did you know this about Charles Wesley: he and his wife Sarah walked that slow funeral dirge march to the graveyard to bury a child five times? They lost *five* children. That funeral dirge must have been playing in their ears as they buried child, after child, after child. And yet something in the power of God's message of resurrection struck at the heart of Charles Wesley's life in such a way that he could write these words:

> *Lives again our glorious King, Alleluia!*
> *Where, O death, is now thy sting? Alleluia!*
> *Once he died our souls to save, Alleluia!*
> *Where's thy victory, boasting grave? Alleluia!*[3]

That's the music of the second line—the second line of hope, the resurrection hope that comes into our lives in the midst of despair. Those despairing moments cannot outlast God's hope. Claim it for yourself, for no one is beyond hope. Not one of us is beyond the reach of God to bring redemption, new life, and hope into our lives.

Second line resurrection music is the national anthem for citizens of hope, empowering us to go forth into each new day as second line singers!

When we can't see
our way out,
God's hope,
God's second line
music of resurrection,
begins to ring
in our ears.

Love Leaves Behind More than Death Takes Away

What else do we hear in the second line music of resurrection? Love leaves behind more than death can ever take away from us. Death does not have the last word. God's love wins.

When we lose loved ones, when we face death, all we can see is the darkness. The Gospel of John tells us that Mary and the disciples went to the tomb early on the first day of that week, "while it was still dark" (John 20:1). That is one of our favorite lines in the New Testament. What was God doing while it was still dark? God was at work in resurrection and new life, "while it was still dark."

While the darkness was still upon them, God was raising up his Son, Jesus Christ, teaching us once and for all that death will never have the last word. That word will always be a word of new life, resurrection, hope. We put our hope in the God of resurrection, with that second line music ringing in our ears. God can use your life and my life, no matter what big messes we've made of our lives. God can take the ravages of our lives—the dust, the wreckage, the ugliness of our lives—and make beautiful things out of the brokenness of our lives.

(Clayton) People ask me if I really believe in the Resurrection. I suppose there are many of us who have had doubts. After all, we have known people who died, and they didn't come back to life and walk among us. Could this story of Jesus rising from the grave be real? When people ask me that question, I always invite them to first look at the biblical witness and recall how the disciples—who were ready to run away, deny their connection to Jesus, and hide—were transformed by their experience of the risen Christ. They left completely convinced that God had indeed raised Jesus, and were willing to put their lives on the line for it. Ask yourself, would I put my life on the line for something not true?

Then I encourage people to look around them to see that resurrection is not just about what happens after we die, though certainly it gives us the assurance that death is not the end. It is also about what God is doing in our world here and now. In every church in which I've served, I can point to people whose lives have been devastated by death, sorrow, and tragedy. Sometimes it has come in the death of a child, a spouse, a sibling, a parent, or a friend. For some it is financial misery and ruin. For some it is the death of a dream. Whatever the situation, I have watched so many people, who thought their lives were over, not only find life again, but become the second line musicians who help others find life again. They are living reminders to me that you can try to nail love to a tree and bury love in a tomb, but God will raise love up. God is a God of resurrection, and yes, I do believe!

Do you believe? Jesus said, "I am the resurrection and the life. Those who believe in me, even though they die, will live, and everyone who lives and believes in me will never die" (John 11:25-26). The resurrection message is what second line living is all about!

(Clayton) Many years ago I was visiting my parents and ended up in my father's study. He had a glass-top desk and underneath the glass I saw a small handwritten note that said, "Love leaves behind more than death takes away." I asked him about it, and he said, "It is the summation of the gospel, the message of Easter. When all is said and done, God's love wins." For him it became a personal statement of his faith. Since that day, I have used that phrase at almost every memorial service I have conducted. It is a phrase that has come to take on a great deal of meaning for many members of the church I serve. It is so important in the face of death to be reminded that nothing, not even death, can separate us from love. When all is said and done, God's love remains.

Here is the challenge for all of us: how can we, those of us who claim to be citizens of hope, begin to put this message of hope into action? Our world is filled with the music of the first line—funeral dirges being played on the airwaves of the evening news, talk radio, newspaper, magazines, and the Internet. So many prophets of doom are preaching the bad news. They say, "There is no hope, all is lost." Who will be the messengers of hope to share the good news with the world?

More than ever, our world stands in need of Christian men and women, young and old and in between, to remind people of this message: in the midst of the gloom and despair we are experiencing all around us, there is a God of resurrection at work, whose love is stronger than death, or hatred, or anything. This God, who has become real to us in the life, death, and resurrection of Jesus, is a God of hope and new life.

Do you know someone who needs this good news today? Will you share it?

God, you are the source of resurrection and new life. Sometimes I am overwhelmed by fear, despair, and the reality of death. Remind me again that in raising Jesus you have sent the second line music with the beautiful lyrics of faith, hope, and love. Help me to hear that music in the midst of my own grief, and the struggles that I face. Because of the Resurrection, strengthen me to live as a citizen of hope, in the midst of a world that often seems hopeless. Challenge me to go out and sing the song of resurrection to those in despair. Thank you for raising up your Son for me and for the world you love. I pray this in the name of Jesus Christ. Amen.

 **REFLECT**

⚓ Port of Entry

Reread John 11:25-26 and John 20:11-18 (see page 86).

The Gospel of John's account of the resurrection of Jesus centers on Mary Magdalene. "Early on the first day of the week, while it was still dark . . ." (John 20:1). John's language speaks not only to the physical reality that the sun has not yet risen, but also the spiritual state of Mary, whose grief is so deep she cannot see that the Son has indeed risen. Her lack of recognition is exactly what grief and other harsh realities in life do to us. But when Jesus calls her by name, Mary, once blinded by grief, can now see. She goes forward to proclaim the good news, the music of the second line, telling others of the Resurrection.

Have you ever heard the risen Christ call you by name?

How does the resurrection of Jesus make a difference in your life?

✍ Customs Declaration Form

What insights did you gain from each section of this chapter?

Living the Resurrection Faith

Faith Overcomes Fear

Hope Outlasts Our Despair

Love Leaves Behind More than Death Takes Away

✪ Passport Stamps

What is "stamped" on your heart that you will remember most from this chapter?

NOTES

Chapter 1: Identity Crisis: Hope in Tough Times

1. "Jesus Is Just Alright with Me," Arthur Reynolds, *Tellin' It Like It Is*, Universal Music Publishing Group, 1966.
2. Jim Collins, *Good to Great: Why Some Companies Make the Leap...And Others Don't* (New York: Harper Collins, 2001), 85.
3. Ibid.

Chapter 3: Fed by Hope

1. "A Service of Word and Table I," *The United Methodist Hymnal* (Nashville: The United Methodist Publishing House, 1989), 10.
2. Ibid.
3. Ibid, 7.

4. "Blessed Assurance," Franny J. Crosby, 1873, *The United Methodist Hymnal* (Nashville: The United Methodist Publishing House, 1989), 369, stanza 1.
5. "A Service of Word and Table I," 10.

Chapter 4: Second Line Living

1. "When the Saints Go Marching In," traditional American gospel hymn, early 1900s.
2. "Will Ye No Come Back Again?" (also known as "Bonnie Charlie"), Carolina Oliphant (Lady Nairne) (1766–1845).
3. "Christ the Lord Is Risen Today," Charles Wesley, 1739, *The United Methodist Hymnal* (Nashville: The United Methodist Publishing House, 1989), 302, stanza 3.

ACKNOWLEDGMENTS

(Clayton) So many people have helped give shape to the formulation of this material. Writing with my sister, Mary Brooke Casad, has been and continues to be a joyous experience. She is one of the most creative, dedicated people I know; a person who truly strives to live her faith in word and deed. Many of the stories we use to illustrate the Scriptures in The Basics series come out of our family experiences in both joyful and trying times. You are a blessing!

I'm grateful to the Worship Team and staff of First United Methodist Church, Richardson, Texas, who helped develop the sermon series in which some of these messages originally appeared, and the congregation who first heard these messages and gave good feedback. Jennifer Rawlinson and Drew Presley were helpful early on in the process with sermon transcriptions. I am always thankful for the many mentors who have blessed my life, particularly my preaching mentor, Dr. Don Benton, and preaching professor, Dr. Zan W. Holmes, Jr.

My wife, Lori, and children, Erin, Katy, and Grant, continue to bring so much joy to my life. They have put up with my writing and offered gracious feedback as well as constant encouragement and support. Thank you all for blessing my life!

(Mary Brooke) I'm profoundly grateful for the opportunity to coauthor The Basics series with Clayton, who besides being my biological brother is a true brother in Christ. His genuine faith is lived out authentically in every aspect of his life, bringing blessing and joy to me and to many others. Thank you, Clayton!

Our stories reflect the blessings of family, friends, and communities of faith who have enriched and shaped us. Except for our family members, the names of other persons in our stories have been changed. I give thanks to God for all who have been a part of my faith journey.

With gratitude for their support, encouragement, and love, I offer my heartfelt thanks to my husband, Vic, and our family: Carter, McCrae, Melissa, Revol, Patrick, and Ana. (And a special word of thanks to McCrae for assisting with the transcriptions of his uncle's sermons!)

We both gratefully acknowledge Neil Alexander and the wonderful folks at The United Methodist Publishing House. A special word of appreciation goes to Susan Salley and Sally Sharpe. Thank you!